The Search:
Calling A Pastor

Rev. Robert W. Legg, Sr.

This book was printed in the United States of America.

To order additional copies of this book, contact:

Rev. Robert W. Legg, Sr.
330 Winding Ridge Dr.
Dayton, Ohio 45415

rlegg1@woh.rr.com

FWB Publications
Columbus, Ohio

FWB
Publications

TABLE OF CONTENTS

❦

"The steps of a good man are ordered by the LORD: and he delighteth in his way. Though he fall, he shall not be utterly cast down: for the LORD upholdeth him with his hand. I have been young, and now am old; yet have I not seen the righteous forsaken, nor his seed begging bread... For the LORD loveth judgment, and forsaketh not his saints; they are preserved for ever: but the seed of the wicked shall be cut off... But the salvation of the righteous is of the LORD: he is their strength in the time of trouble,"

--Psalm 37:23-25, 28, 39.

❦

PREFACE

Someone told me one of our conference "sister churches" had hired a new full time pastor. Perhaps a week passed and I called to introduce myself and welcome him to the area. Within a few short moments he was crying, and stated God knew he needed to talk to someone.

He had moved his family across two states and several hundred miles to accept the position as pastor. During his visit(s) with the church he did not discuss salary and did not get the housing issue clarified. He was told simply the church would "provide" adequate housing and would give him a "good" salary.

He was married with two children, an eight year old son and an eleven year old daughter.

The housing turned out to be a very small apartment with two tiny bedrooms. The kitchen and living room area covered about a ten by sixteen foot area. His salary was $250.00 a week.

It was impossible for him to pay his bills, school his children and feed his family.

My wife and I provided food, took them out for meals, and sought help for them through the conference , which really worked to try to improve the situation.

Who was wrong in this arrangement? Neither party. No one was wrong, neither was right, either.

ROBERT W. LEGG, SR.

The church, not having had a "full time" pastor thought they were doing right. The pastor did not clarify his needs or the churches intents because he did not want to give the impression he was accepting the position just for money. He trusted the church to do right. The church thought they did.

I've thought many years about this situation. The young pastor had to drive all night after Sunday evening service to get "back home" where he worked in timber all week, driving back on Saturday for services Sunday, until he could get enough money to move his family back to his home state. He was very bitter toward the Free Will Baptist churches and ceased trying to pastor. Shame.

-- Rev. Robert W. Legg, Sr.

PURPOSE OF THIS BOOK

I'm writing this work, hopefully, to help both our churches and prospective pastors in their endeavors to make informed decisions. There should be no surprises for either the church or the new pastor after the office of pastor is assumed.

I am also aware that these suggestions and views will draw criticism. Some, perhaps, even severe. That's OK. I understand the nobility of the calling to pastor. I understand the propriety of church government. But, between the ideal and the ridiculous we find the majority of pastor/ministers and churches. It is to these majorities I address these issues. I would love to say , "I have all the answers." I don't. I do, though, have some opinions. In my thirty years of pastoring I have encountered a myriad of problems, met lots of good – and bad – people, and do know that I wish I had known when I began at my first pastorate what I know now. It would have made my journey easier.

It is for that reason I write this. Perhaps it will assist some pastoral candidate and maybe some church from experiencing unnecessary problems.

I fully believe both ministers and churches want to do the right thing. Doing the right thing has to start somewhere. That's where we begin.

You may feel, reading through the following suggestions and statements, that the relationship between church and pastor is a "we-them" attitude. Confrontational.

It is not. Or, rather, it isn't supposed to be, and in most cases it is not.

With deep respect these two parties – church and pastoral candidate – should prayerfully address one another with the simple goal of discovering God's will for the two of them in this search.

I've tried to delve deeply into the search process and bring out as many issues as possible so both parties can approach each other with questions that, if asked and answered, will avert that confrontational or regretful probability later .

There are books and pamphlets out there covering these issues. I have read only one of them, and that after completing the first draft of this work. That publication was *"Calling a Pastor"* by Rev. Bob Shockey, Randall House Publishing, 1974. He covers points I do not. I would recommend obtaining a copy of his work to see those suggestions. If any of the things I suggest coincide with any points made by others it is purely by coincidence.

SECTION ONE

DISTINCTIONS

Before listing the suggestions for the church seeking a pastor it is necessary to make the distinction between" full time" and "part time" churches. It, also, becomes necessary to subdivide the "part time" churches.

A "full time" church is one, naturally, that employs a pastor in a "full time " capacity. It is his only job. The church provides a salary and benefits to support the pastor and his family.

A "part time" church is one that , naturally, is not "full time", but instead, has a pastor that supports himself primarily through a secular job. This pastor is limited in the time he can devote to the church. Most of the Free Will Baptist churches are "part time."

In the family of "part time" churches several differences arise. There are "part time" churches that try to compensate the pastor with some regular pay for his services, there are those that designate one or two Sunday offerings a month for the pastor, there are those that take up a "love offering" for him (which is recognized by the IRS as an income that must be fully declared, although most churches and most ministers are not aware of the law). There are some which offer no compensation.

Sadly, there is a third group. There are churches that not only do not believe a pastor should be salaried, but they are also of the opinion that, regardless of the size of the congregation or responsibilities of a pastor, he is to be "part time" only.

I visited one particular church with nearly three hundred people regularly attending that absolutely refused to consider having a full time pastor. They are good people. They have just been taught, somewhere, by someone, that it is un-Biblical.

They have never been able to understand why they can only keep a pastor for a short time.

They burn them out.

It is just not possible for a man to work a 40 hour a week job, be a father and husband, fill the pulpit three services a week, and tend to the needs of all the people in a church of that size.

How is a man supposed to visit the sick, be with bereaved families, preach funerals, comfort people having surgeries , and their families , counsel, attend special programs, perform pre-marital counseling and weddings, and attend conferences and board meetings of a church with a large congregation, while at the same time attending to work and family?

Either his health, his sanity, or he, will leave. There is no choice.

The needs differ between "full time" and "part time churches". The expectations differ. The requirements for a pastor differ. These factors should be kept in mind as these suggestions are reviewed.

People differ, churches differ.

There are differences between locations.

Differences in style, differences in worship, differences in goals.

SECTION TWO

THE CHURCH

SUGGESTIONS FOR THE CHURCH SEEKING A PASTOR

First, where do you want to go and what do you want to do as a church? You have either just lost your pastor or he has notified you he is leaving. Don't wait for an emergency situation during the vacancy in your pastorate to decide you need to do something. If your by-laws don't provide for a pulpit/search committee, the leadership board(s) of the church should immediately confer and decide on your direction. Your desired direction will help determine the qualifications you will want in a new pastor. A review of your budget and expenditures will show you what you have to work with for salary and benefits.

The longer a church goes without a pastor the longer someone, or some persons, in the church will have to make critical decisions. Sadly the longer this continues the more entrenched that person or those people will become in that duty and they are very likely not to want to surrender that authority to the new pastor, or they will contest with him for power. If the church has a strong board , already established, and already involved, as a group, to handle issues, this will be either minimalized or non-existent.

Before you call the first candidate, determine if you are going to commit yourselves to working with the new pastor to either move the church forward or continue its movement forward. A pastor cannot do all the work necessary to see a church grow. He needs help. His job is to "steer the rudder". The job of the church, and especially the leadership, is to "pull the oars."

ROBERT W. LEGG, SR.   11

1. **Know the type of pastor you want and need.**

   A. **Full Time or part time**

   In most cases this difference is merely a matter of semantics. Most of the "part-time" pastors I know are as committed to their church in time, study, and leadership as most "full time" pastors. They are excellent men of God and care for His flock.

   If you can afford to support a pastor with sustaining full time salary, do so. You will benefit by having a pastor whose time is devoted undividedly to your church.

   If your circumstances dictate you must have a part time pastor, that's OK.

   It takes ten full time wage earners paying tithes in a church to provide adequate revenue to support a full time pastor. That is over and above ALL the other financial responsibilities of the church being met. So, if you don't have that, or if the church does not have some other source of continual sufficient income, think part time until your situation changes.

   Keep in mind that a part-time pastor must divide his time between the church and his regular 40 hour a week job. Knowing this, if you do decide on a part-time pastor , consider, and respect any free time he has or may need with his family.

   B. **Qualifications.**

   Although churches should demand belief and commitment to Free Will Baptist doctrine, other issues can be ambiguous. An undergraduate or graduate degree ? No degree? There are men with degrees and men without degrees who cannot do a good job pastoring. You are not looking for a piece of paper.

ROBERT W. LEGG, SR.

You are looking for a qualified person to shepherd your church. Remember, all pastors are ministers of the Gospel. All ministers of the Gospel are not called to pastor.

You would do well, though, to seek the most dedicated Bible student, the best read individual, the most literate and articulate person available. The higher the education achieved the more likely these qualities will exist, but be sure to consider the experience and pastoral ability.

C.   **Preaching style**.

Men differ. Styles differ. Churches have preferences.

The content of the message should be more important than the delivery.

A candidate for a particular church presented the Greek words for a couple of the KJV words in the text, and gave their meaning, which not only changed the context of the verses, but expanded and made more dynamic the intent of the writer. One was saved and a young couple rededicated in the service. The church told the candidate they were afraid to hire him. They were afraid they would be getting a "teacher" and not a "preacher. "

Concentrating on the "preaching" of a minister and not his pastoral abilities has been the bane of many churches.

Sometimes churches just have no idea what they want. Sometimes what they think they want is not what they need. Pray and be sure.

2. **Compensation**

A.   Know what the church can afford in compensation before calling anyone as a candidate.   There are several things to consider. First, what are the church's financial obligations.

They must be met first. It is recommended a budget is used to give clear information of income, regular operating expenses, and discretionary monies.

A church may not like the thought, but they are a business. They are involved in a Holy work. Every effort should be taken to account for every penny received and spent. It is God's money.

An account of how it is used will be demanded. Handle finances as a business. If a church does not understand how to handle finances and how to manage its operations it will have problems.

B.   Know the salary you will offer, the benefits you can provide.

The "rule of thumb" is that the full time pastor should be paid no less than the average salary of the working people in the church. A church should not expect their pastor to have to live on less than they do. He has a family, and bills, too.

I tell this in humor. As a candidate for a church I was asked "What will It take for you to come here?". I replied, "What do you think is fair?". One of the deacons replied," My father was a pastor. I know what they have to do and what they need. Besides a living salary, I would like for you to have an educational allotment for continued studies, a clothing allowance, since you are representing not just God but this church, an automobile allowance, and a book allowance. I would also like to make a contribution to the retirement fund. But since we can't afford all that right now, this is what we can begin with as a salary." He was straight forward. I liked that.

Know what you can pay and the benefits you can provide.

If your church does not have enough people with sustaining full time jobs to establish an average starting salary for the pastor, then you are probably not financially sound enough to properly support a full time position. You need to seriously consider a part time pastor until the church grows to a place it can easily afford a full time salary.

Part time churches will not have all these problems with salary, but they should be aware of the expenses a pastor has. I pastored one church for over six years with no pay. They did begin putting a little each month into a fund for me to use to purchase books and supplies.

A church asked a minister to help as an interim (which turned out to be a stay of nearly seven years)

They offered him three hundred a month for expenses. And, even then , a couple quit attending.

When visited by the interim and one of the deacons the couple clearly said they left the church because they felt the minister had come there just for the money.

There are at least four causative factors prohibiting churches from either being financially sound or from providing support.

The first, and most obvious, is either a congregation too small or too needy to provide the revenue.

Secondly, and probably one of the most unbiblical reasons : the belief that accepting or providing any monies from a church is dealing "filthy lucre."

Thirdly, an attitude on the part of primarily the pastor that the church is too poor to provide any assistance. This is a result of a simple failure.

When a pastor does not teach tithing and free will offerings to the people it is a fair guess he does not practice regular giving himself.

ROBERT W. LEGG, SR.   15

Fourthly, and obviously, the failure of the church to teach and practice tithing. Paul wrote in 1 Cor. 16: 2, "Upon the first day of the week let every one of you lay by him in store, as God hath prospered him, that there be no gatherings when I come." Other passages supporting tithing are Deut. 16:17; Rom. 12:8; 2 Cor 9:7; Acts 11:29; Lev. 27:30 (which says that tithes are holy); and the most direct, Mal. 3:10.

As a church, as a pastor, search your hearts and make sure you are Biblical in teaching, giving, and receiving tithes, and wise in the expenditure of that which now belongs to God.

That brings us to this point. It does not matter what you, as a church, agree to pay the pastor, someone will complain that it is too much.

Do what is right. Jesus said in Matt. 19: 9-10, "Provide neither gold, nor silver, nor brass in your purse. Nor script for your journey, neither two coats, neither shoes, not yet staves: for the workman is worthy of his hire."

Paul wrote in 1 Cor. 9:14, " Even so the Lord hath ordained that they which preach the gospel should live of the gospel." His writings in Gal. 6:6 and in Phil. 4:14-16 reaffirm this position.

Know the **salary and benefits** you can and will provide before beginning your search. Be in agreement as a board and as a church. It is bad business to try to negotiate salary and benefits with a candidate only to have to take the proposal to the church for open discussion and approval.

It is wise for the pulpit/search committee to have the permission of the church to resolve these issues in conference with the candidate. Let him know that once the decision is made to call him, all negotiated issues are automatically confirmed.

ROBERT W. LEGG, SR.   16

Some churches grant the authority to hire the pastor to the pulpit/search committee. Most reserve that right to be decided by a vote of the church in an open business meeting.

Regardless of the procedure followed by your church, let the candidate know during the interview process .

Continuing education. The more a pastor grows intellectually the deeper he is likely to become in Scripture. He will become steadily better as a minister, a pastor, a person. Consider paying for or assisting the pastor to continue his studies.

Book Fund: It is not uncommon for a studious pastor to amass a library of tremendous cost. Consider providing a regular amount of money for him to draw from to purchase books and material.

Conferences, seminars, retreats, state, and National Association meetings.

A pastor needs spiritual renewals. He also needs to be current with Denominational trends and issues. Try to cover these costs.

Automobile. It is not unreasonable in some areas for a pastor to travel several hundred miles a week visiting hospitals, shut ins, and attending to appointments with the people or for the church. It may sound like a lot, but it is not. The payment for an economical auto is not much and a card for gas and expenses should be easy to provide. People are not aware of the diner and coffee meetings a pastor has with ministers, business leaders, and church prospects.

Pension fund. Few churches consider that at some point it is very likely a man must retire. The people in the church want to eventually retire.

They fail to take into consideration that most pastors make such a small salary they just manage to provide the basics for their family and are not able to pay into a retirement account. That means when the pastor is no longer able to pastor because of health or age, he has absolutely no income.

Some pastors pay into social security, but that is not a sufficient retirement income for most, and definitely not retirement income enough to permit any more than, perhaps, a small amount necessary to live on. Ministers have the option of paying into social security or not. Some do not simply because they cannot afford to lose 13% out of their pay. That means they will have zero pension.

Pray hard about paying into a retirement program for the pastor.

The FWB Board of Retirement has an outstanding program and they will be very happy to both provide adequate information and assist you in your decision and efforts.

Housing.

If you are calling a full time pastor you will most likely hire someone who must relocate. That means he will need housing for himself and his family. Most ministers do not have the funds to purchase a new home . If the church provides a parsonage, remember that the pastor MUST pay taxes on the rental value of the house. If the church covers the utilities, taxes must be paid on that, also. Make sure the salary is sufficient for him to be able to pay these additional taxes without burden.

If the church does not have a parsonage, or if the new pastor obtains his own housing ,then a housing allowance needs to be considered. A housing allowance does not have to be reported and poses no immediate tax burden on the pastor. He must keep records of expenses for presentation if audited. Should the allowance be less than the actual expenses, he will pay no taxes. If the allowance is greater than expenses he will be liable for taxes on the differences. It would be well for the church, and the pastor, to obtain a copy of current tax laws for ministers and churches to ensure compliance with changing laws.

Moving expense.

If it is necessary for the new pastor to relocate, be prepared to cover the cost of the move.

Also, be prepared to give the pastor and his family assistance in finding adequate housing. Remember, he is probably new to the area, does not know the neighborhoods, does not know where to look or what to expect.

Don't call a pastor and just leave him and his family to find housing by themselves. They are under a tremendous burden just moving and beginning a new ministry with you. They could use all the help possible to lessen the already stressful situation.

2.   The questions

Take the time to prepare a list of questions for the candidate(s).

You may want two lists.

The first one to serve as a filter so you can focus your time on just those candidates you feel best for the church. Don't be shy. Ask.

It would be advisable to clearly state the church's expectations of a new pastor in the preface of this questionnaire. Let the candidate(s) see and fully understand what you want of them before they commit themselves to your review process.

You want to know through these questions if a minister meets, at least, the minimum requirements you desire in a pastor.

For example, you might ask questions.

(1) Personal:

Married? Who? When? How long? DO you or your wife have a living spouse? Children? Ages? At home?

(2) Religious experience:

Where, when saved?

Explain your call to preach

Where, when licensed, ordained.

Affiliation with a church? Conference?

(3) Experience:

Work experience, qualifications other than the ministry?

(4) Ministry:

What ministries, where? When?

How long?

(5) Education:

List schools from High School through graduate. What classes? Degrees?

Develop you own list of questions. From the answers given here you can determine if you want to look more closely at the candidate. This is the time to ask the hard denominational questions. Ask for references.

Give this list to the candidate(s) immediately upon contact with them.

Have it returned to you as soon as possible, review it quickly, and decide if you want to look closer at the candidate(s).

The second list of questions would be asked the candidate during the interview process with the pulpit/search committee.

Now you want to ask about ministry goals. It is here you can determine, to some degree, the candidate's thinking process, depth of knowledge, stand on issues, theology, problem solving, and cooperative nature.

These questions might include:

(1) How would you work with boards? Deacons?

(2) Do you hold in confidence conversations? Counseling sessions?

(3) If there is a problem in the church, who should handle it? How?

(4) What support would you give existing ministries?

(5) When would you plan to make changes?

Again, be inclusive. This is God's church but YOU have been given the responsibility of finding the one man God wants to lead you and the rest of your flock. Don't be so fast you miss the obvious; don't be so slow you weary the process. Be clear. Be concise. Have a purpose for each question.

3. Calling the minister

Resume Reviews

When a church receives a resume they should be careful not to jump to too many assumptions. For instance, any minister having left a church (or churches) will be very careful with his wording about that church. Instead of counting the churches a man has pastored (as a negative quality), count the number of pastors that church has gone through. A lot of times God sends a man into a difficult church to help correct a problem. Sometimes it is to give him more training for the "next" church. Sometimes the church is such a problem no one can overcome the issues. Most ministers will stay away from problem churches, if they can, because they know it might tarnish their reputation if they fail. Some pastors are used by God as "firemen" who have the job of going to problem churches and battling through the hard issues for the sake of the church and the good people who are there.

Don't write a man off just because he has been at different churches.

Remember this: the experience you need from a new pastor might not be taught in a school. Age is not always a bad thing.

Check references before you call a man. Pray about him

Once you call a man as a candidate, concentrate on him and him only.

Remember, you are not in a grocery shopping for a piece of fruit or a ham for dinner. Don't look at two or more ministers at the same time trying to determine which looks the best. If you call a man, concentrate on only him.

CD or No CD? DVD or no DVD?

Some churches like to have candidates send a cd, DVD, or a tape to listen to before asking the man to come for a personal visit. I know they believe it serves as a filter, but I don't believe it does. It actually is detrimental. If they believe they can decide on the type of preacher they want simply by listening to a taped message, then they are using the wrong criteria. A tape cannot always relay the intensity or impact a message has. It cannot duplicate the Spirit that accompanied the message. It can reveal the man's diction, perhaps the content of his (one) message.

If you are drawn to a man by his resume, call him and listen to him in person.

Advertise

For churches seeking a full time pastor, it would be well to let your needs be known broadly. There are some services available, like FWBPastor.com, or some state association assists. It would be a great if there was a central service provided on the national level to cover notifications from churches needing pastors. The South Carolina Association of Free Will Baptists does an outstanding job serving as a clearing house for churches in that state seeking a pastor.

Have a point person

Have one person on the committee appointed as the contact person. They should be the one to make appointments with candidates, and see that all the arrangements are made, pickups arranged, thank you letters written. They don't have to do all the work but they need to make sure it is done, and they should be the one making the appointments and contacts.

Pre-plan the visit

First, be prepared to cover the cost of the man visiting your church. He will most likely bring his wife with him, too.

Arrange for a place for them to stay, a nice hotel/motel or a good family from the church. Make plans to cover all their meals. Allow them some free time to talk. Arrange for their transportation. If it is far, fly them.

Don't forget to give the minister an honorarium for preaching.

I know there are those reading this who will say that these suggestions are too much of a financial burden on a church.

Let me ask a question. Would you expect less from an employer wanting to hire you?

A pastor is no less a person, no less a provider for his family, and deserves no less than an average salary.

If a church cannot adequately pay these expenses, then it should seriously consider whether it can afford a full time pastor.

The Interview

Allow time for the search/pulpit committee to speak with the candidate. Have your questions planned ahead. This is a serious discussion for you to make a determination whether you would like this man as your pastor . It is not an inquisition.

It is very disturbing for a minister to sit as a candidate before a committee and be questioned or treated without respect. This is a minister of the Gospel.

Before the meeting is over, find out how soon the minister can relocate if the church calls him.

ROBERT W. LEGG, SR.   24

Allow the candidate to present his questions to the committee and the church. It is advised he present his questions to the committee before coming for the interview to give the church time to properly answer them. As a church, you don't want to be caught off guard by a question. You are not only looking for a pastor you can be comfortable with, but the candidate is also looking for a church he feels he can minister to. Both of you have to be at peace with ALL the issues that are brought up.

Fellowship Time With The Church

The people need to get to know the candidate. Obviously there is little time for sufficient casual interaction to permit learning a lot about the man, his wife and family, but make time to learn what you can. If it is possible, plan on the church having a fellowship diner following the morning worship service. Give the people time to greet and speak with the candidate. This ,also, gives the candidate time to learn something about the people of the church.

If the candidate is known to the congregation it may be felt this diner is not necessary. Do it anyway. It will tell the candidate he is coming to be more than just a "preacher"; he is coming to be part of the church family.

Act Timely on Each Candidate

Following the visitation, hearing him preach, and the conference, make a decision whether to present him to the church for a vote. If you choose not to place him before the church, let him know as soon as that decision is made. It is advisable to waive the rules for scheduled business meetings. If the search/pulpit committee recommends a man to the church for vote, that decision should be before the church the next Sunday following morning service.

It is unfair to the ministers, and to the church, to "look at" several men before trying to come to a decision. Ministers in such a situation are put in the position of having to "compete" with other ministers, which is wrong, and the church is left in absolute confusion because they cannot filter all the information given them.

Look at one man and make a decision on him. Yes, or no. If "yes" the search is over. If "no", then look at another man and repeat the process – yes or no.

Closing the File

Lastly, closing the file on a minister. PLEASE take time to contact every minister that submits a resume to your church. Let him know where the church is in its search and let him know if he is still being considered . Notify each minister when a decision is made. Thank each minister that has contacted your church for showing a concern for the church and the office of pastor.

SECTION THREE

THE PASTOR

B. **Considerations for the Minister**.

There is a serious burden on a church seeking a pastor to make sure they are in the will of God with their choice.

There is no less a burden on the minister.

Most ministers being considered for a part time position know the church, the congregation, and the community, He probably knows the history of the church, the past problems, and the current issues. His desire is to serve and to help the church. He will usually be a local with friends and family in the church. He usually is a fine man and a fine choice.

The same is not always true for a full time pastor. He may not be from the area, may not be familiar with the history of the church, current issues, leadership, the real government (not what is written in the By-laws, but how things are really run), teacher selection, church financial condition and commitments, expectations, customs. These are things, among others, that are well worth finding out before deciding on accepting the position. Which means they must be asked. He, too, is usually a good man seeking God's will.

Don't be afraid to ask hard questions. Better to ask them before accepting a position than wishing you had afterward. All churches are not the same. All are not managed the same. Most people serving on operating boards of churches are not professional managers. They are mostly honest every day working people trying to serve God and their church. Differences are inevitable.

I had assumed the position of part time pastor for a great congregation. I could see that the offerings were good. The business reports supported my observation. The only problem was that the bank account did not reflect a strong balance. Some work needed to be done on the church and there was insufficient funds. I asked if the offerings had been that "good" for any period of time and was told they were. When I asked what happened to the funds, I was told, simply, that every time anyone from ANY ministry visited the church and asked for support, someone would ask "How much money do we have?", then make a motion to give the ministry a great portion of it. The church was not wrong in wanting to help, just not wise in the way they did it. Their first responsibility was to see to the wellbeing of their facility and provide for a viable outreach in their community. We incorporated a by-law that allowed 10% of our income (the tithes on our tithes) to be allocated for causes outside the church. It was subdivided for different state and national offices and ministries. It actually permitted us to become a greater supporter of those ministries than prior to the change. It worked.

Churches have good intentions. Some just need direction.

In one (full time) church, all available funds – which meant everything in the bank - was at the total discretion of the trustee board to use as they pleased.

The new pastor did not know this before taking the position and it created difficulties when he asked for simple things, like a much needed file cabinet or for material for non-existent visitor's packets. They refused to allocate the money.

It wasn't that they did not have the funds, they did. They were just showing their new pastor who actually had the final say in the church.

Be aware of this. If a person or a single group or board makes all the decisions regarding all the expenditures of a church, you will be walking into a definite situation where the decision making and power of the church rests with this person or group. The power is not in the open discussion and decision making of the church and definitely will not include input from the new pastor.

Who controls the money holds the power.

I've watched church board members use the power of the purse to abuse and seriously mistreat a pastor. I've seen them keep him just above starvation in income so they could flex their "Look at me, I'm someone with authority" muscle.

When God established the order of relationships in the Bible, He did so for a purpose. He wanted, and wants, order and propriety.

The first relationship responsibility is to be between man and God; the second is to be between a man and his wife and family. The third relationship is between man and those outside his family. That means that before you, as a minister, commit yourself and your family's wellbeing to a church, you ensure that the welfare of your family is properly taken care of. They are your responsibility before the church. If you cannot manage the needs of your family you definitely cannot manage the needs of a congregation.

Understanding the differences possible, I asked one church that had interviewed me for a copy of the previous year's business meeting minutes, along with a copy of the treasurer's reports. Those two reports would have allowed me to see how their business was conducted, what their priorities were, and how their finances were handled. They would not furnish me the reports. I did not go there.

Again, it is better to get the answers before taking a position than stepping into a financial and operational quagmire. You must remember your and your family's wellbeing are at stake. It is your responsibility.

I would suggest you obtain a copy of the By-Laws of the church for which you are a pastoral candidate. Also, obtain copies of minutes of business meetings and copies of treasurer's reports. From these you will easily understand the church's operating principles, financial status, philosophy, fiduciary behavior, and responsibility.

Prepare a list of questions you want to ask the search/pulpit committee. Don't be afraid to "get into their business." If you become their pastor it will be your business, or rather, the system within which you must do business.

Expect the church to cover the expense of your visit as a candidate. It is their responsibility. If they cannot afford to cover those expenses, they cannot afford a full time pastor .

I was called by a church and asked to come as a candidate for pastor. When I mentioned I would have to drive there on a Friday to be rested for Sunday (an 11 hour drive) and that I would have to find a place to stay, I was told they would see me when I got there. My flag went up. After the trip, the visit, the services, and no mention of covering the expenses, I just left and drove home. That trip took longer because of the traffic. I was disappointed. Not at the loss of money, but at the church. I sent a letter thanking them for permitting me to be with them and politely suggested that for any future candidates they consider covering their expenses. Although I was out over $500.00, I told them I did not want a reimbursement. I received an e-mail from the deacon offering an apology and telling me he was sending a check for part of my expense.

He stated the church was unable to repay me for all the cost. The event and message told me the church would not be able to cover any moving expenses, help with housing, and really could not afford an acceptable salary. In other words, they could not afford a full time pastor. These were, and are good people with good hearts. They deserve a good pastor who will love and serve them. They just cannot afford a full time pastor at this time. Perhaps later.

The Resume

Prepare a professional level resume.
I would advise keeping one on file and always updated.

There are many resume programs available that lead you easily through the construction process.

In addition to the personal, educational, and professional information you will provide on the resume, consider including a statement of your beliefs and a brief statement of your goals as a pastor.

References:

Before listing anyone as a reference, contact that person, explain to them what you are doing and obtain their permission to submit them as a reference. I know you have friends you feel would not object to being listed, but be courteous and contact them anyway. It isn't that they mind being listed; they just need to know.

ASK QUESTIONS

The following is a list of sample questions you might consider asking. It is not all inclusive and is offered as only an example.

Sit down and make your own list of questions. Pray about them. Dig. Try to learn all you can before making any commitments. Remember, when you realize you are up to your neck in alligators, it is too late to remember your first responsibility was to drain the swamp.

Drain the swamp.

1.   What is the church's policy on time off during the week?

(At one church I was told Sunday counted as one of my days off. Really?)

2.   What is the policy for vacations?

This is important for your wellbeing as well as the good of your family.

You need to get away. Your wife and children need, and deserve, the special family time a vacation brings.

3.   What is the policy for family emergency, ie. Death, hospitalization?

(At one church following the death of a parent I was given the option of taking the time off without pay or using vacation time. This should not have been)

4.   What goals does the church have for its future?

"Without a vision my people perish".

ROBERT W. LEGG, SR.

5.   What programs would the church like implemented?

From this question you can learn whether they are forward thinking.

6.   What part will church leadership and members play in the implementation of programs to achieve the stated goals?

In other words, "what help will I get from the church and the church's leadership in setting goals and working toward them?"

7.   What is the policy for selection of teachers and the Sunday School Superintendent?

Some churches have well established Education departments or boards that work earnestly to ensure the best and most qualified teachers are in place. Some determine those positions through popularity vote. In some churches the positions are filled by appointment. You need to know this.

8.   Does the church cover the pastor's expense to State Association meetings, the National Association meeting, and in-state retreats (FWB men's fellowship) and training sessions?

9.   What is the salary review policy?

No one would take a secular job that did not have a salary/pay review policy. Inflation affects a pastor's salary, also. Sadly, most churches have no review policy. As a candidate you may not see the importance of this, but believe me, after being at a church for several years without either a raise or even the discussion of one, you will not only see your purchasing power severely diminished, but you will also conclude easily that the church does not consider you, your family, or your ministry there important. It is hard to keep the sails up when there is no wind.

10. Does the church provide basic cell phone service for the pastor?

Nearly 95% of calls received by a pastor are church related. This is a reasonable request.

11. What duties are expected of the pastor, other than the common duties of study time, sermon preparation, lesson preparation, visiting the sick and shut-in, visiting visitors, soul winning, preaching, counseling, weddings, funerals, church fellowship, general overview of the church and shepherding the flock?

12. What does the church expect the pastor's wife to do?

Remember, her FIRST responsibility is to be your wife, the mother of your children, your helper in the Gospel. She is your "helpmeet", not an assistant pastor.

13. What are the church's response plans in case of emergency? Have they been discussed with local law enforcement and fire services?

Do you have evacuation charts posted? Do you have emergency teams trained to assist with first aid needs? With directing the people to exits.

14. What steps are in place to provide congregation security?

The ultimate safety of the church rests in your leadership. If the church has not done anything to define and plan for emergencies, you will have to direct them in that task. Today's unstable world says that things will happen and says that you MUST protect your people.

It is better to plan comprehensively for an event that never occurs than to witness a tragedy that could have been averted.

15. Are church insurance guidelines and recommendations followed regarding regular background checks on all persons working with children, and providing a safe and abuse free venue for children?

Most churches are totally unaware of recommended, and, in some places or with some insurance companies, required protective measures.

16. What is the frequency of church business meetings? What are the guidelines for presenting items of business to the church?

17. Do you operate with a budget, and if so, how is it determined?

The smallest churches should learn to prepare and operate with a budget.

It permits closer scrutiny of income/expenses and helps eliminate wasteful spending. Remember, again, once that offering is received, it is ,EVERY PENNY , God's and is to be used extremely wisely.

18. How many pastors have you had in the last 20 year? How many years did they serve? Why did they leave? (This may sound strange, but there are churches – especially in rural areas, that believe 2 or 3 years is enough for one pastor. It affords no opportunity to accomplish anything and gives no security to the office).

19. Do you have a soul winning, outreach program? Would you support an active one?

20. How is church direction and philosophy determined?

In other words, how is the church's belief system determined? How is its witness and reach into the community decided?

ROBERT W. LEGG, SR.

Who develops the plans for the future growth – both spiritually and physically - and ministries of the church?

21. Does the church believe in, teach, and support tithing?

If it does not, it will never be sound financially. Tithing is not, as some advocate, a money issue. Tithing is a spiritual issue. It is, also, an obedience issue.

22. What is the church's stance on the doctrines of the Free Will Baptist?

We are experiencing critical times. There are Free Will Baptist church that are not recognizable as such because of their shift in doctrine. There has always been the problem of other denominations infiltrating Free Will churches, primarily via ministers/pastors, with the goal to lead the congregation into different beliefs. They have been successful in many cases. They continue the practice.

A Free Will Baptist church should believe and teach ONLY Free Will Baptist doctrine. Know what you are getting into.

Personally, I feel that people, or denominations, that infiltrate and lead congregations out of the Free Will doctrine are committing simple theft. They are taking something they did not work for or build. The Bible I use makes a clear statement about that. Paul wrote in 1 Cor. 6: 10 "Nor thieves….shall inherit the kingdom of God."

23. Should the National Association, the State Association, or the Central District ever change its position on issues that, to this point, have been Biblically and properly defined as sin, what action would the church take?

24. What is the church's position on abortion? On gay rights? On consuming alcohol? Cohabitation?

There should be absolutely no difference between Scripture and the church's position on any of these matters.

25. Would the church support cross-cultural evangelism?

We are in an ever changing and more diverse culture than ever. It is imperative the church be ethnically inclusive to be relevant in the community in which it is located.

26. Who is responsible for church maintenance? Janitorial duties? Lawn care?

An important question?

Yes.

You don't want to assume a pastoral position just to find out the church expects you to be the all-around handyman., too.

If you don't mind that, fine. But be aware of two things. First, it is not fair for a church to demand so much from a pastor. His time is limited as is. Secondly, akin to the first, it will definitely lessen the time you will have to properly accomplish the duties for which you were originally hired.

27. Is the Treasurer bonded?

28. How many signatures are required on a church check?

For safety, and security, it is recommended that there are always at least two signatures on a church check.

I would strongly suggest that all churches review some of the published procedures for handling church finances. It can prevent a host of problems.

One that I would recommend is "Safeguarding the Financial Assets of Your Church" published by the Indiana Conference of the United Methodist Church. It is concise, easy to read, and on point. It is also available online. Just Google it.

29. Do you conduct audits at least annually?

This is a continuation of the previous question.

30. Do you have a Building Fund? Benevolent Fund?

How are they funded? How are they managed? Who manages them?

It would surprise you to learn how many churches are not meeting 501(C) mandates for donations and expenditures.

31. What type of service do you prefer during mid-week? Sunday evening?

Someone wrote that those who attend Sunday morning service love the church; those who attend Sunday evening service love their pastor; those who attend Wednesday service love God.

I strongly feel our people need more than forty-five minutes of church a week.

32. How often does the church hold Communion/Foot-washing?

Simple. If we are Free Will Baptists, be Free Will Baptists.

33. Do you have a New Convert's training class?

The problem of seeing people "come in the front door and go out the back" has some to do with them being quickly grounded in the faith. If there is no program, one needs to be established.

These type of questions just let you know if the church is active in the pursuit and maintenance of souls or if you have another job to attend to if you should go there.

34. Do you have a welcome packet for visitors? What is your follow-up program for visitors?

35. Do you have Greeters on Sunday morning for visitors?

First time visitor to a church decides within a few minutes of entering the building whether they will return or not. That is before the first song and before the message, It all depends on the aesthetics, and the comfort they feel from being received in the church.

36. What is the church's policy about weddings in the church?

Churches differ on what they permit or don't permit. Find out.

37. Does the pastor have final say in the usage and filling of the pulpit?

Imperative.

38. Are the deacons of the church committed to supporting the pastor in fulfilling his duties to the church and in fulfilling the Great Commission?

39. What roles do the deacons in the church fill?

We all know the Biblical instructions for the role of the deacon. The problem, in a lot of our churches, is that that role has morphed into something the Bible does not mention.

For instance. After going to one church I discovered the interim had "set aside" six men for examination as deacons.

I have a policy. Even after discussion with the board and approval of the church and the setting aside of a prospect, I require them to attend a six session class on the "Duties and Responsibilities of a Deacon." I want to be sure they understand their role.

Upon meeting with the six men for the first session, I just asked each one separately, "What would be your primary responsibility as a deacon?". One of the men matter-of-factly looked me in the eye, pointed a finger at me, and said, "My job is to make sure you teach and preach what you are supposed to.".

He did not become a deacon.

It is amazing that in most of our churches the congregation has no problem voting a pastor out just because he perhaps combs his hair wrong some Sunday morning, but they keep deacons for life who misuse their office.

Know what you are getting into.

40. What is the Sunday School Department doing to grow the Sunday School attendance?

A church is either growing or it is dying. Church growth is best accomplished through the Sunday School and through an active soul winning program. They must work together.

41. What are youth leaders doing to grow that ministry and expand youth involvement in the church?

Probably the greatest challenge for today's church is the evangelism, training, and incorporation into the church body, the youth.

It requires a concerted effort. IT IS IMPERATIVE.

42. Does the Clerk send "thank you" cards to visitors?

Often this is all that is needed for a person to decide to return to the church.

43. It does absolutely no use for a pastor to preach, teach, and beg for people to get involved, grow in grace, be faithful to the church in all areas, including attendance and tithing, if church leaders and teachers do not set the example.

Are the leaders and teachers in the church setting the example for new people and the youth in attendance? Holiness? Ministry involvement? Tithing?

Do their lives demonstrate true Godliness?

Do they show genuine love for the brethren in the way they deal with issues? Gossip? Differences?

(This may be the one question that defines the church)

44. Do the people in the church come to worship God , learn, and grow ?

I won't say anything negative about some changes being made in a lot of our churches. I firmly believe they are being made because the pastor and the congregation feel they are necessary. I just hope commitment to holiness, commitment to Godly worship and music are not compromised in the process. There is a balance that must be maintained.

Primary to all that happens is the sincere preaching of the Word of God. Necessary are the messages that "edify" the saints. Necessary are the messages that point the lost to the Christ of Calvary. Necessary is the music that glorifies God and not man.

45. Will the church cover moving expenses?

I overheard a couple deacons from a church talking about their past pastor. He had been with them over fifteen years. They were persistent in their aversion that the church had helped with his moving expenses when he first came. That is a shame.

There are not many ministers looking for a pastorate that have several thousand dollars sitting idly in the bank waiting for them to take out to pay for moving their family across country to accept a position. Most are either broke or near broke.

The church should readily, and happily – without negative remarks as noted above- pay for the move.

46. What is the starting salary and benefit package offered?

If you find the offer not sufficient, negotiate.

You have to pay your bills, feed, and clothe you family out of this salary.

Make sure it is sufficient.

As a candidate for a church I countered the church's offer.

The difference was $23.87 a week. They called and said they were going to continue their search for a pastor, they felt they could not afford me. A church board that will not negotiate freely is one that probably has an issue with pastoral authority. Or one that will want to micro-manage the pastor.

They demonstrate, like the church above, that it is either "their way or no way."

47. How many young couples or Millennials, do you have?

Ministering to this group is particularly challenging and absolutely necessary.

Often inordinate emphasis is on the "youth" movement and great attention is given the "seniors", but this group is neglected. It is not by design. It is just assumed that this group requires less "maintenance" than the others. That is not true. If anything they require more. Addressing them, their spiritual needs, and their church involvement is different and more demanding that the other groups. But to keep them and to see that group grow, you need to be specific in your ministry to them.

THE FOLLOW UP

Following the selection of a pastor, the job is not finished.

Some things to watch for:

Churches, and especially church boards, will tell you a lot about themselves, their issues, sacred cows, power issues, ability, and willingness to learn, support and grow, their love for God and His church, the sweetness of their character. All these, and more, can be learned by asking the right questions, carefully analyzing the answers, watching and listening during meetings and times of fellowship at what both is said and not said, watching body language and eye movements, and above all, listening to the voice of the Holy Spirit.

Earlier we addressed the issue of who controlled the money controlled the power.

This needs to be addressed, again, in another direction.

I want to give a heads up to ministers seeking a pastorate about a much known, yet seldom spoken about, condition found in, too often, too many churches. It is churches controlled by a specific family, person, or power group. We are not talking about church under a well-defined and operating board of directors or general board. We are talking about unwritten yet assumed control of a church.

Unless you adhere to the pleasure of that person or group you will not survive at the church.

Unless that power is broken and properly returned to the church body you will not see progress.

If you don't want to have to fight to change the situation, don't go.

If you do go understand you are already handicapped. You will have to work hard, and perhaps long, to garner the support of the rest of the church before even attempting to change the situation. And don't fool yourself. The rest of the church body are friends, and perhaps relatives, of the power broker(s). You are the outsider. Regardless of how close you think you might be to those people; you are the "new guy." Don't get trapped.

Often an effort to change is futile. You are likely to get emotionally and psychologically bruised. Your ministry might be injured.

Find out.

Talk to pastors you know in the conference. Ask if they know of any particular issues in the church you should know about before you make your decision.

Watch and listen (We've covered this before but is it of most importance).

Most churches do not have major issues plaguing them. But, if they do, and if after finding out, and after God has confirmed His desire for you to go there, by all means GO. God is telling you that He is tasking you with the responsibility of leading His church in the right direction. He will lead, the Holy Spirit will encourage, and glory will result.

Lastly, for the minister, PLEASE send a letter of thank you to those churches inviting you for an interview. Every interview will not result in a pastoral job but every interview should be appreciated. The church has shown respect to you. Return the favor.

Follow up

For the Church:

If the pastor is new to the area, take the time to have someone show the pastor and his family the community.

Provide him and his family a "welcome basket" with a few essentials like coffee, milk, bread, eggs, cereal, etc. Enough for just a few days until they get unpacked and settled.

Help him find important places,: government offices, license bureaus, food stores, drug stores, banks., schools.

Remember, he and his family need the fellowship of the church to assist them to settle. Invite them for coffee and cake. Take them for ice cream.

Be patient with him and his family as they acclimate themselves to the new church, a new community, a new home.

They have left friends, and perhaps family, to be with you. Understand that at times they may get "homesick". Help them to feel that now THIS is their home. Don't tell them. Show them.

Following the selection of a pastor, the job is not finished.

It is at this point, if agreed upon, a full contract between the new pastor (full time) and the church would be drafted. A contract not only delineates expectations and goals, but establishes a high degree of security for both parties.

For the new pastor:

Sit down with boards and committees, department heads as soon as possible. Learn how they operate and what they are doing, what are their goals, needs. Your job is not to change them. Your job is to understand them so you can help them move forward in their ministries. They will be the spearhead of your future ministry there. Establish an immediate working relationship with them.

Meet with the different church groups as soon as possible; senior's, ladies auxiliary, Master's Men, Youth., etc. Again, learn what they are doing so you can give proper support and, if needed direction.

And, for you. Have patience with the church, also. Just as you are trying to learn them, they are trying to learn you. Some may seem to push; some may seem aloof. They just don't know you personally and need time to discover who you are and how you react to them.

CONCLUSION

There is no greater a blessing than being called of God to pastor. There is no greater a responsibility – souls are at stake; church welfare is at stake.

The qualities and abilities of a pastor differ greatly from those of an evangelist. The messages are different, their purpose different.

A pastor must be an administrator, a leader. He must be an organizer, a motivator.

The union of a church with a new pastor is more than filling a job. It is the merging of philosophies, a commitment to a unified purpose, an agreement to Biblical standards for growth and cooperation.

Most of our churches have "part time" pastors. I've been one. It is not easy. But the blessings are no less. We have some very good churches, full time, and part time. We have some very good people in both.

There are issues, yes. One of the primary problems many of our churches is defined by the statement, "Well, that's the way we've always done it."

Another is, "We don't like change."

In an interview with a pulpit committee I asked the question, "Do you like where you are as a church and where you are now headed?" They responded they did not like either, but that they didn't like change ,either. My response was simple. "If you continue doing things the way you are, you will not only stay in the condition you are in but continue in the direction you are going. It will get worse. It is your choice."

ROBERT W. LEGG, SR.   49

A pastor's job is to love the people, edify the saints, minister to the needs of the congregation, give a doctrinal foundation to new converts, be an administrator, train leaders and workers, direct a viable outreach for souls, and help the church get a clear vision and move in the right direction for strength and growth. His job is to equip the members of the church to be living witnesses of God's grace in the community , to be souls winners, to be true light in a dark and sinful world, to be life changers. Be honest, be open, be focused, BE DIRECT. It is not a job for the faint of heart.

The church's job is to provide the platform for the pastor to serve, and to pray for and to cooperate with the pastor in those endeavors

As a church seeking a pastor, pray before you choose.

As a minister under consideration for a pastorate, pray before you commit.

Notes

_____

_____

_____

_____

_____

_____

_____

_____

_____

_____

_____

_____

_____

_____

_____

_____

_____

_____

_____

_____

_____

_____

_____

_____

_____

_____

_____

_____

_____

_____

_____

_____

_____

_____

_____

_____

_____

_____

_____

_____

_____

_____

_____

_____

_____

www.ingramcontent.com/pod-product-compliance
Lightning Source LLC
Chambersburg PA
CBHW060623030426
42337CB00018B/3172